Should School
LUNCHES
Be Free?

By David Anthony

KidHaven
PUBLISHING

Published in 2018 by
KidHaven Publishing, an Imprint of Greenhaven Publishing, LLC
353 3rd Avenue
Suite 255
New York, NY 10010

Designer: Seth Hughes
Editor: Katie Kawa

Cover © istockphoto.com/SolStock; p. 5 (top, background) StevePell/iStock/Thinkstock; p. 5 (top, inset) © istockphoto.com/asiseeit; p. 5 (top, girl) gmstockstudio/Shutterstock.com; p. 5 (bottom) monkeybusinessimages/iStock/Thinkstock; p. 7 Ariel Skelley/Blend Images/Getty Images; p. 9 SolStock/E+/Getty Images; p. 11 Tupungato/Shutterstock.com; p. 12 (main) fotoedu/iStock/ Thinkstock; p. 12 (bread) Eising/Photodisc/Thinkstock; p. 13 courtesy of the Library of Congress; p. 15 Kathryn Scott Osler/The Denver Post via Getty Images; p. 17 Monkey Business Images/ Shutterstock.com; pp. 19, 21 (inset, middle-left) wavebreakmedia/Shutterstock.com; p. 21 (notepad) ESB Professional/Shutterstock.com; p. 21 (markers) Kucher Serhii/Shutterstock.com; p. 21 (photo frame) FARBAI/iStock/Thinkstock; p. 21 (inset, left) XiXinXing/iStock/Thinkstock; p. 21 (inset, middle-right) Africa Studio/Shutterstock.com; p. 21 (inset, right) XiXinXing/Getty Images.

Cataloging-in-Publication Data

Names: Anthony, David.
Title: Should school lunches be free? / David Anthony.
Description: New York : KidHaven Publishing, 2018. | Series: Points of view | Includes index.
Identifiers: ISBN 9781534523326 (pbk.) | 9781534523340 (library bound) | ISBN 9781534523333 (6 pack) | ISBN 9781534523357 (ebook)
Subjects: LCSH: School children–Food–Juvenile literature. | School lunchrooms, cafeterias, etc.– Juvenile literature. | Children–Nutrition–Juvenile literature.
Classification: LCC LB3475.A6465 2018 | DDC 371.7'16–dc23

Printed in the United States of America

CPSIA compliance information: Batch #BS17KL: For further information contact Greenhaven Publishing LLC, New York, New York at 1-844-317-7404.

CONTENTS

Free
FOOD

Lunchtime is a fun part of the day for many students. It's also an important time. When students eat a healthy lunch, they get the **nutrients** they need to grow and stay fit. For some students, lunchtime is the only time during the day when they eat a healthy meal. They get their lunch for free because their families have a hard time paying for food.

Is it a good idea for schools to offer free lunches? Some people think it is, but others don't agree. These people have different opinions. It's good to understand different opinions before forming your own.

Know the Facts!

The United States Department of Agriculture (USDA) is the part of the federal, or national, government that controls free lunch **programs**.

Should school lunches be free for everyone, some students, or no one at all? It's helpful to know all the facts before deciding what you believe.

A Lunchtime
HISTORY LESSON

Some students bring a lunch from home to school. Many others, though, get a lunch that's made for them at school. These lunches cost money, which is often paid by students or the adults who care for them.

In some cases, the money needed to pay for the lunches comes from the government. In 1946, the National School Lunch Act created the National School Lunch Program (NSLP). This program provides free or low-cost lunches to students whose families don't make enough money to afford a school lunch. Taxes help pay to keep the NSLP running.

Know the Facts!

In 1966, the School Breakfast Program—also known as the SBP—started as a way to provide breakfasts to children who didn't have healthy food to eat at home.

Some people think free lunch programs should be **expanded** beyond the current NSLP to include all students. There are many reasons people support and oppose this idea.

Fighting Food
INSECURITY

Children need to eat enough healthy food as they grow, but sometimes that's not easy. In 2015, 13.1 million children in the United States were considered food insecure, or without enough **nutritious** food on a regular basis. Millions more children come from homes that aren't food insecure but still struggle to provide them with three healthy meals every day.

Free school lunches help these children get at least one healthy meal every weekday. For some students, a free lunch could be the only food they eat all day.

Know the Facts!

The NSLP also helps schools provide free, healthy snacks to children and young adults in afterschool programs.

More than 30 million students **qualify** for the NSLP.

"No Such Thing as a FREE LUNCH"

The NSLP provides free lunches to students who need them, but some people believe in the old saying, "There's no such thing as a free lunch." Although the lunches may be free for students in need, someone has to pay for them.

The government provides the money for free lunches, but it gets the money from taxpayers. Some people believe it's not fair to ask people to help pay for someone else's lunch. Others worry that the United States is in too much **debt** already and shouldn't pay more money for things such as free lunches.

Know the Facts!

It cost $12.6 billion to run the NSLP in 2014.

Some members of the federal government believe the NSLP wastes government money. They think it needs to be fixed so people who don't really need free lunches can't get them.

Making Healthy
CHOICES

Those who support the NSLP state that it provides students with more than just free food; it provides them with free, healthy food. In 2010, the Healthy, Hunger-Free Kids Act was put in place. This act set nutrition standards for free meals in schools.

These standards were **designed** to help fight childhood **obesity** by giving children healthier food options. Students who eat healthy lunches have more **energy** and do better in school than students who are hungry or eat unhealthy meals.

Know the Facts!

The NSLP's nutrition standards call for more fruits, vegetables, and whole-grain foods, as well as only low-fat or fat-free milk.

Former First Lady Michelle Obama played a big part in making sure school lunches met nutrition standards to help all children stay healthy.

Wasting a Healthy
LUNCH

Although the nutrition standards set by the Healthy, Hunger-Free Kids Act have many supporters, others don't approve of them. They believe the government shouldn't control what kinds of food children eat.

People who argue against free lunches for students also note that healthy food isn't always the food children want to eat. Studies have shown that students end up throwing out large amounts of the fruits and vegetables they're supposed to take with their free lunches. This wastes food instead of helping students form healthy eating habits.

Know the Facts!

A 2015 study stated that students were throwing away 56 percent more fruits and vegetables than they were before the Healthy, Hunger-Free Kids Act.

Some people don't see the point in having free lunches if students are going to waste the food they're given.

No Longer SINGLED OUT

Some people believe school lunches should be free for all students—not just those whose families can't afford it. Students who get free lunches sometimes feel singled out for having less money than other students. This leads some who need free lunches to refuse to **participate** in free lunch programs. They don't want anyone to know they need help paying for meals.

Making school lunches free for all students would make sure no child feels different because of what they can or can't afford. It would help students see each other as equals.

Know the Facts!

Detroit and Boston are two U.S. cities that offer free lunches to all students in their public schools.

Free lunch for all students is also known as universal free lunch.

Problems with Universal FREE LUNCH

A service called the Community Eligibility Provision (CEP) allows schools in **low-income** areas to provide free lunch and breakfast to all students. If a certain amount of students in an area qualify for free lunch, then all students get free lunch.

Many people have argued against this service. They believe that if there are some students in these areas whose families can afford lunch, those students shouldn't get lunch for free. People who oppose CEP believe the government and taxpayers shouldn't have to pay for lunches for kids whose families can afford it.

Know the Facts!

CEP was part of the Healthy, Hunger-Free Kids Act of 2010.

Should students get free lunches if their family can afford to pay for their meals?

What Do YOU THINK?

It's important for students to eat healthy meals. It helps them do well in school and grow into healthy adults. Some students wouldn't get a healthy meal without their schools' free lunch programs, but not everyone thinks these programs are worth the money they cost.

People have made strong cases for and against free lunch programs. After learning the facts, what do you think? Should school lunches be free? If you think free lunches are a good thing, should they be free for everyone?

Know the Facts!

The Summer Food Service Program provides free meals to students when schools are closed for the summer.

Should school LUNCHES be FREE?

YES

- A free lunch might be the only food a child eats in a day.

- Free lunches help fight food insecurity.

- Free lunches provide nutritious meals that help students perform better in school.

- Universal free lunch programs help students who feel singled out for needing free lunches.

NO

- The U.S. government's debt is too high to be paying for lunches.

- Taxpayers shouldn't have to pay for other people's lunches.

- Free lunch programs lead to wasted food.

- Universal free lunch programs waste money because not every student who's part of the program needs a free lunch.

When forming your opinion about the need for free lunches, it's helpful to consider both sides.

GLOSSARY

debt: The state of owing money.

design: To create the plan for something.

energy: The power to work or to act.

expand: To become bigger.

low-income: Not having a lot of money earned through work.

nutrient: Something taken in by a living thing that helps it grow and stay healthy.

nutritious: Having things that people or animals need to be healthy and grow properly.

obesity: The condition of being very overweight.

participate: To take part in something.

program: A plan or system under which action may be taken toward a goal.

qualify: To meet a required standard.

WEBSITES

National School Lunch Program (NSLP)

www.fns.usda.gov/nslp/national-school-lunch-program-nslp
This website features information about the NSLP, including its history and nutrition standards, that comes straight from the USDA.

School Lunches: KidsHealth

kidshealth.org/en/kids/school-lunches.html#
Visitors to this website find tips for making healthy lunch choices whether you buy a lunch, bring a lunch, or get a free lunch.

BOOKS

Allman, Toney. *Food in Schools.* Chicago, IL: Norwood House Press, 2014.

Bloom, Paul. *Rules at Lunch.* New York, NY: Gareth Stevens Publishing, 2016.

Reinke, Beth Bence. *Nutrition Basics.* Minneapolis, MN: Core Library, 2015.

INDEX